# THE HISTORY OF
# TRANSPORTATION

**BRIAN WILLIAMS**

Thomson Learning
New York

# CONTENTS

First published in the United States in 1996 by
Thomson Learning,
New York, NY

Published simultaneously in Great Britain by Wayland (Publishers) Ltd.

Library of Congress Cataloging-in-Publication Data
Williams, Brian, 1943–
    The history of transportation / Brian Williams.
        p.    cm.—(Science discovery)
    Includes bibliographical references and index.
    Summary: Provides a general history of transportation including
wheeled vehicles, boats, airplanes, and spacecraft.
    ISBN 1-56847-282-X
    1. Transportation—History—Juvenile literature. [1. Transportation—
History.] I. Title.  II. Series: Science discovery (New York, N.Y.)
TA1149.W31996
629.046'09—dc20                          95-40609

Printed in Italy

*Concept* David Jefferis
*Illustrations* Alex Pang and Peter Bull (page 34t)
*Cover design* Norman Berger, New York

**Acknowledgments**

Environmental Picture Library 40; Life File 4; Michael Holford
6b, 11, 12-13, 18; Peter Newark's American Pictures 9, 14-15,
15, 34, 43 Peter Newark's Historical Pictures 8, 14t, 23, 24b
Quadrant 21, 22-23, 24-25, 28, 28-29, 30, 32-33, 35, 40-41, 45
Science Photolibrary 13t, 36, 38, 39, 42, 46-47; Tony Stone 5,
10, 17, 20, 20-21, 29, 30-31, 37; Zefa 6t

*Cover:* A modern luxury cruise vessel. Courtesy of Renaissance Cruises,
Inc., Ft. Lauderdale, Florida.

# INTRODUCTION

We have been on the move ever since our first ancestors crossed the plains of Africa, hunting and gathering food. They traveled on foot, along river valleys or paths made by migrating animals. By the end of the Stone Age, people were trading in flint, amber, salt, and obsidian. These goods were passed along trade routes, some of them hundreds of miles long.

About 10,000 years ago people in the Middle East, India, and China built the first towns. Farmers sold their crops to townspeople, and for transportation they used tame animals, such as donkeys, to carry loads. Later they harnessed oxen to carts with solid wooden wheels.

Social, economic, and military pressures have made people look constantly for new ways of traveling and moving their goods. We do not know who made key inventions such as the canoe paddle, the sail, or the wheel. These things appeared in different places at roughly the same time. Good ideas passed speedily among groups of people; the evolution of writing around 3000 B.C. made it possible to record details of inventions and pass them on.

◀ Animal transportation, like this camel in Pakistan, relies on muscle power. It does not require any alteration to the environment.

▲ Modern transportation consumes vast quantities of resources. Besides the energy required to build and power these cars, considerable amounts of materials and energy are required to build highways like this one in Los Angeles, California.

Today people want to move themselves and their goods across continents in hours, not weeks. Technology in partnership with science, human need, and ingenuity—backed by money—have created the locomotive, the car, the truck, and the airplane. Modern transportation has provided personal mobility and global travel—but at a cost. In busy cities, travel by car can be slower than travel by horse and cart a hundred years ago. Even the skies are congested.

Machines need fuel, and burning fuel pollutes the air. The fuel used by most vehicles is made from oil pumped from beneath the ground—oil resources will not last forever. In the future, many of our travels may be restricted. Instead we may have to explore through the electronic superhighways that connect computers around the globe.

# THE FIRST BOATS

**P**eople traveled on water long before they took to wheels on land. The earliest boats were log rafts, animal skins filled with air, or canoes made from reeds or hollowed-out trees. Paddles were in use by 8000 B.C. The Inuit kayak and Welsh coracle are both simple, ancient craft. Both use paddles and are light enough to be carried by one person, and both are still in use. By about 3000 B.C. Egyptian sailors had sails as well as paddles to propel their craft.

► Canoes turn over less easily with an outrigger, an extra float fastened to one side. The canoe then becomes a twin-hulled catamaran, a design used for thousands of years by islanders in the Pacific.

Bow

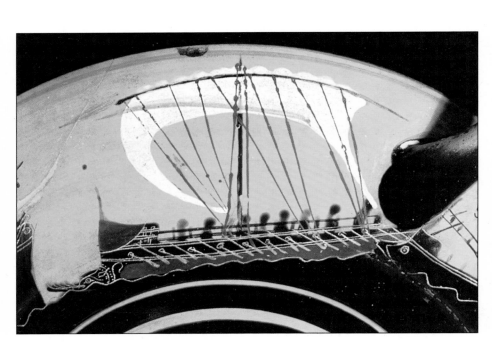

◄ The ancient Greeks sent ships beyond the Mediterranean, as far north as the British Isles and the North Sea. They built war galleys with two or three banks of oars for extra power. These warships had an armored spike or ram in front, to smash into enemy ships. This warship is part of the decoration on a cup made in Athens around 540 B.C.

We know from wall paintings in Egyptian tombs that the Egyptians made boats seven thousand years ago. The Egyptians paddled along the Nile River in slender boats made from river reeds tied in bundles, because wood was scarce. Larger ships had teams of rowers with oars. In 1970 Thor Heyerdahl, a Norwegian anthropologist (1914– ) fascinated by ancient seafaring, sailed a replica of an Egyptian reed boat across the Atlantic Ocean.

This demonstration showed that Egyptian sailors could have voyaged at least as far as the island of Crete, and perhaps farther.

Later sailors built wooden ships, which were bigger and stronger. They are called galleys. Like Egyptian ships, they had one large sail, and when there was no wind, or when navigating a river, they used oars. The galley was steered by a large oar at the stern. In such ships, the Phoenicians (people who lived in what is now Lebanon) explored and traded as far as the west coast of Africa.

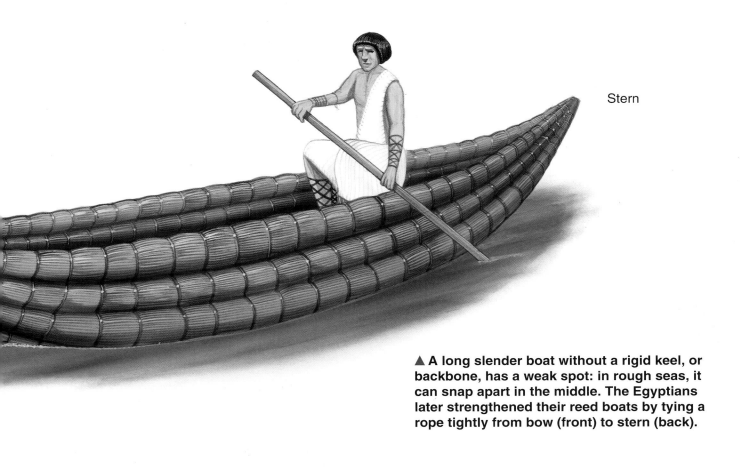

Stern

▲ A long slender boat without a rigid keel, or backbone, has a weak spot: in rough seas, it can snap apart in the middle. The Egyptians later strengthened their reed boats by tying a rope tightly from bow (front) to stern (back).

The Romans used large cargo ships to carry grain and wine. They traded with outlying parts of the Roman Empire, such as Britain. Sailors used their knowledge of wind, tides, and stars to find their way, but they kept close to land as much as possible. Roman cargo ships were up to two hundred feet long. It was a thousand years before other European boat builders could surpass them.

# CHARIOTS AND CARTS

Imagine a Stone Age farmer about six thousand years ago clearing a patch of forest. He hacks at a tree with a stone ax. His companions drag away the heavy branches. By chance, a big log falls across two smaller ones. The men push it, and it moves more easily than when it rested on the ground. Imagine their surprise and delight.

The small logs act as rollers, reducing the friction between the big log and the ground. Log rollers made it possible for people to move huge stones, like the ones at Stonehenge in England. Stone Age people also discovered that a load resting on a board was easier to pull.

Around 3500 B.C., Sumerians living in Mesopotamia (in modern Iraq) were the first people to use wheeled carts pulled by oxen. Their wheels were solid, made from pieces of rounded wood fastened together. There were no iron tools at that time, and stone tools could not slice tree trunks into neat wheel shapes. Early wheels often broke as they bumped over rocky tracks.

The wheel was a landmark idea. It features in most forms of transportation and in many engines and other mechanical and electrical devices. Probably no other single invention has done more to change the way people live.

◄ King Ramses II of Egypt (1304–1237 B.C.) standing in his war chariot

▼ Wagons pulled by oxen played a vital part in the westward expansion of Europeans across the North American plains. The wagons painted here by the artist Dorenceau are shown crossing the Platte River in Nebraska.

## ☀ THE FIRST ROAD BUILDERS

The Romans were the first scientific road builders. They surveyed routes, using a sighting instrument called a *groma*. They dug out the ground and laid a foundation of clay, chalk, or gravel. They added cement and a top surface of paving stones. Roman roads were cambered, or angled, so that rainwater drained off into ditches at the side. They were also very straight. Some modern roads follow the same routes as Roman roads. After the Roman Empire fell in the fifth century A.D., road building in Europe was neglected until the 1800s. A Scottish engineer named John McAdam (1756–1836) built stone-topped roads that, unlike dirt roads, vehicles could use in bad weather. The invention of the automobile, with rubber tires, brought the smooth blacktop or concrete roads of today.

The light but strong spoked wheel evolved in Egypt around 1500 B.C. Short, curved sections (now known as fellies or felloes) were held together by a tire made from metal strips nailed to the wood. Spoked wheels were fitted to two-wheeled carts or chariots. Pulled by horses, the chariot was the first war vehicle.

At first, wheel and axle were fixed so that both turned at the same time. Later, the wheel was held on the axle by a pin, so the wheel turned while the axle did not. Soon after 1000 B.C. four-wheeled carts with swiveling front axles were being used in southern Europe. These made driving around corners easier, but the invention disappeared and did not resurface until around 1350, in the Middle Ages.

Horses were too valuable to pull carts—that work was left to oxen and donkeys. The horse was a war animal, used in battle by charioteers and cavalry. The essentials of a horse harness were the bridle and bit, saddle, and (invented last, about 200 B.C.) stirrups. Horses could not pull heavy loads because neck straps and yokes choked them. About A.D. 800 the horse collar solved the problem, and horsepower dominated land transportation throughout the Middle Ages.

# OCEANGOING SHIPS

Transportation technology in Europe changed little during the Middle Ages (roughly from A.D. 500 to 1500). The Vikings sailed their longships across the Atlantic Ocean to Greenland, and some even landed in North America, but their ships were no more advanced than the ancient Greek galleys. At that time the Chinese built the largest sailing ships in the world. Their seagoing junks had four or five masts and were steered by a stern rudder (Europeans were still using a large oar). The junk's sails, kept flat with wooden slats woven into the fabric, were easy to operate, and some ships had removable masts. The hull was divided into watertight compartments, so the ship was less likely to sink.

◄ Chinese junks are still built in the traditional way with sails that are easy to adjust.

European ship design began to change in the 1400s. A new ship called a carrack had three masts carrying square and triangular, or lateen, sails. The lateen sail, copied from Mediterranean and Arab ships, was easy to swing to catch the wind. Having both types of sails enabled sailors to adapt to changing wind conditions.

Ships of the 1400s were small. When the Italian-born Christopher Columbus (1451–1506) sailed west from Spain in 1492, the biggest of his three ships weighed only 80 tons. Yet in such small vessels, sailors voyaged not only to the Americas, but also to India (Vasco da Gama, 1498) and around the world (Ferdinand Magellan, 1519–22).

▲ This Dutch ship painted by artist Cornelius Verbeeck (1590–1633) is typical of European ships of the sixteenth century.

 # FINDING THE WAY

Out of sight of land, sailors relied on the sun and stars to find their way. The magnetic compass appeared in China by 1100 and in Europe nearly one hundred years later. Medieval sailors used charts known as *portolani*, based on compass readings. When Christopher Columbus set out westward across the Atlantic Ocean in 1492, he was misled by wildly inaccurate maps. He thought that a few days' sail would bring his ships to Asia. Instead he landed on islands to the east of a massive continent hitherto unknown to Europeans. During the 1500s, maps improved and sailors could measure the height of the sun above the horizon using instruments such as the astrolabe and the backstaff. From the height of the sun, a navigator could calculate how far the ship was from the equator (its latitude). Estimating position east or west (longitude) was difficult until, in 1761, English inventor John Harrison (1693–1776) tested the first reliable sea clock (chronometer) on a voyage to Jamaica.

▼ To find a ship's latitude (distance north or south of the equator), sailors often used an astrolabe. This instrument measured the height of stars, by which sailors estimated their position.

In the 1500s much bigger ships were built. But designing ships was still a craft, not a science. Shipbuilders made drawings, but relied mostly on rough measurements and experience. If a rich person ordered a new ship bigger and more showy than any built before, it was built—even if the result was dangerously top-heavy.

▲ The log was used to measure speed. It was thrown over the stern with a very long knotted line attached. The number of knots that went over the stern in one hour gave a measure of the speed in knots: 1 knot equals 1.1508 mph.

# THE STEAM REVOLUTION

Until the 1700s, the only way of doing heavy work was by using muscle, water, or wind power. A Greek inventor, Ctesibius of Alexandria, made a pump for water in the second century B.C. It used a piston that moved up and down inside a cylinder. Piston pumps worked by hand or animal power were used through the Middle Ages to pump water from wells and mines. In 1698 an English engineer named Thomas Savery built a steam pump to remove water from flooded mines, but without great success.

Fourteen years later the first working steam engine was invented. Like Savery's pump, its purpose was to remove water from mines. The inventor was English blacksmith Thomas Newcomen (1663–1729). His engine condensed steam in a cylinder, creating a vacuum, which pulled a piston down. The piston was attached to one end of a beam, which rocked up and down like a seesaw. The other end of the beam was attached to the piston of the pump in the mine. The Newcomen engine was reliable and commercially successful, though inefficient. It had no challengers for 60 years.

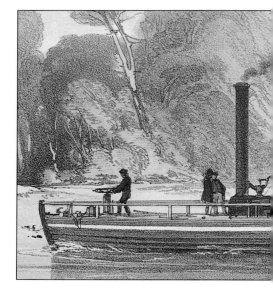

▼ Symington's steamboat *Charlotte Dundas* was tested in Scotland during 1801 and 1802. It was intended as a tugboat on the Clyde–Forth Canal but never went into service.

## THE CANAL BUILDERS

The first canals in recent times were built in Great Britain. They had a golden age for a few brief years at the beginning of the Industrial Revolution in the late seventeenth century, when they were the main means of transportation for bulky materials. The canal builders, engineers like Thomas Telford (1757–1834) and James Brindley (1716–1772), were largely self-taught.

The canals fell into disuse because the steam engine was quickly adapted to run on rails and proved a cheaper way of moving freight. The long water routes across Europe, Asia, and the United States, however, are still in use today. In the United States, the St. Lawrence Seaway links the Atlantic Ocean with the Great Lakes as far as Duluth, Minnesota, 2,323 miles inland. It was a joint U.S. and Canadian project to build 182 miles of canal deep enough to take oceangoing vessels; the project was started in 1954 and the canal opened in 1959.

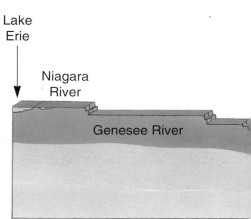

Lake Erie

Niagara River

Genesee River

James Watt (1736–1819), a Scottish engineer who worked as a technician at Glasgow University, became interested in steam engines after repairing a Newcomen engine. Watt could see ways of making improvements and finally patented his own steam engine in 1759. Further modifications and patents followed, and by 1781 he had an engine that could drive wheels around and around, rather than drive a beam up and down. The engine had a flywheel, a crank, and a spinning governor to control its speed. It was ready to drive the factory machines and vehicles that would spawn the Industrial Revolution.

▲ James Watt perfected a steam engine in 1781.

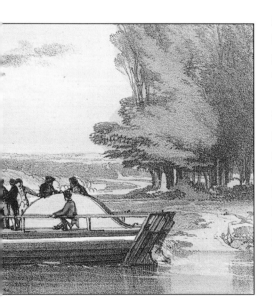

A French engineer named Nicolas Cugnot (1725–1804) made the first steam-driven vehicle in 1769. It moved—slowly—but crashed into a wall and was locked up for everyone's safety. Steam engines performed much better on water. A steam-driven paddleboat was made in France in 1783 by Marquis Jouffroy d'Abbans (1751–1832). In 1785 in the United States, inventor John Fitch (1743–1798) built a model steamboat with wheels on the sides. In 1802 Scottish engineer William Symington (1763–1831) completed the first workable steamboat ever built: the *Charlotte Dundas* was intended as a tug to pull barges along the Forth River and the Clyde Canal in Scotland. The first regular steamboat passenger service began in 1807 on the Hudson River in New York, when the *Clermont* chugged its way from New York City to Albany. The steamboat had been built by Robert Fulton (1765–1815), an American engineer. It was so successful that steamers built under his patent were used on many American rivers.

◄ The Erie Canal joined Lake Erie to the Hudson River. Opened in 1825, it covered 363 miles and had 83 locks. The chief engineer, Benjamin Wright (1770–1842), knew little about canal building at the beginning of the project, but he set high standards and trained his workforce on the job. He became the acknowledged American expert on civil engineering. The Erie Canal had fallen into disrepair, and when it was restored it was some 15 miles shorter.

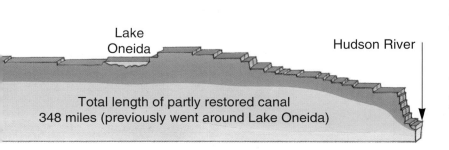

Lake Oneida

Hudson River

Total length of partly restored canal 348 miles (previously went around Lake Oneida)

# THE FIRST RAILROADS

Speed of travel did not matter much before the 1800s, but the Industrial Revolution, the age of factories and machines, changed this. Factories swallowed fuel and raw materials by the wagonloads every day. They poured out goods in unimagined numbers—goods that had to be moved as fast as possible to ports and cities.

Mineworkers long ago learned that moving coal cars was easier if the wheels ran on wooden or iron rails. In 1804 Richard Trevithick (1771–1833), an English mining engineer, took a steam engine from a steam drill and got it moving on rails. His locomotive pulled a load of ten tons at five miles per hour. Trevithick built a steam carriage for passengers, and by 1814 several steam trains were working in coal mining sites in northern England.

▲ Richard Trevithick's steam engine was on trial in London in 1808. Although Trevithick was an ingenious inventor, he was not a very good businessman: he died penniless.

▶ The Central Pacific Railroad was built eastward across the United States starting from Sacramento, California. Thousands of Chinese laborers were hired to blast out ledges along the steep sides of the Sierra Nevada.

Among the engineers making steam engines were British inventors George Stephenson (1781–1848) and his son Robert (1803–1859). In 1825 a locomotive built by the Stephensons traveled from Stockton to Darlington, England, on the world's first public steam train. The train was made up of wagons and carriages normally pulled by horses. The Stephensons then built an engine called *Rocket*, which won a speed competition to work on the Liverpool-to-Manchester railroad. The first passengers were carried in 1830, amid great excitement. But the grand opening was marred by the train fatally injuring one of the officials.

▼ **The Central Pacific Railroad joined with the Union Pacific on May 10, 1869 in Promontory, Utah. The Union Pacific was built westward from Omaha, Nebraska. The joint railroad was nearly 1,800 miles long.**

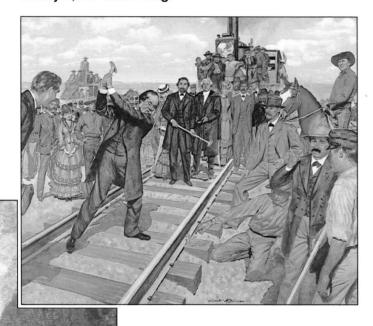

The speed with which railroads were built was astonishing. Railroad fever spread across the United States and Europe, and by 1854 it had reached Australia. Locomotives grew bigger and faster. Extra wheels spread the weight of larger boilers. At first, accidents were all too common. Air brakes (1869) and signaling systems made train travel safer. Gangs of laborers laid track across mountains and deserts. They bored tunnels, raised embankments, and built bridges. Trains drove into the hearts of cities, to elegant new stations—fitting homes for the puffing monsters of steam. For the first time, people could travel faster on land than a horse could gallop. They could send goods by train, go to work by train, and travel on vacation by train. It was a revolution that changed the way people thought about time and distance.

# BALLOONS AND AIRSHIPS

**O**n November 21, 1783, amazed Paris citizens watched a yellow-and-blue taffeta globe rise into the air. From a basketwork gallery below it, two men waved. One was a scientist named Jean de Rozier, the other an aristocrat named the Marquis d'Arlandes. The world's first "aeronauts" were flying, in a balloon filled with hot air, built by the Montgolfier brothers: Joseph (1740–1810) and Etienne (1745–99). Few in the crowd understood what they saw; to them it was magic. People had flown toy balloons before, but no one had built one 65 feet high and able to lift two people.

**T**he Montgolfier hot-air balloon was quickly followed into the skies by balloons filled with hydrogen gas. This lighter-than-air gas had been discovered in 1766 by English scientist Henry Cavendish (1731–1810). French physicist Jacques Charles (1746–1823) flew a hydrogen balloon in France on December 1, 1783. He made the hydrogen by pouring sulfuric acid onto iron filings in a barrel of water. Filling the balloon took four days but the gas balloon soared to 10,000 feet, high enough to give its brave pilot a headache.

▲ The Montgolfier balloon rose in the air because a fire below the open mouth of the balloon heated the air inside. The air inside expanded, becoming lighter than the air outside and making the balloon rise.

▼ The *Hindenburg*, built in 1936, could carry 72 passengers in great luxury. Passenger quarters were inside the gondola and there was even a dance floor. Four large diesel engines produced a speed of almost 90 miles per hour.

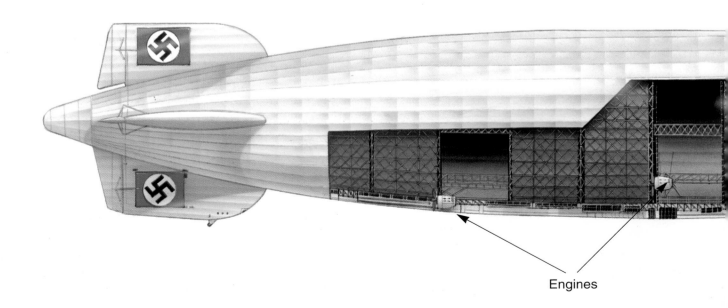

Engines

In the 1800s balloonists made news. They crossed seas and mountains. They did stunts, gave joy rides, and jumped wearing parachutes. They flew above battlefields to spy on the enemy. But balloons go only where the wind blows them, and attempts to steer them with oars or hand-turned propellers proved useless.

In 1852 French engineer Henri Giffard made a cigar-shaped balloon with a steam engine that turned a propeller. This was the world's first airship. In 1885 an airship was fitted with one of the new gasoline engines. Gas engines were developed by German engineers Gottlieb Daimler (1834–1900) and Karl Benz (1844–1929), who were busy building the first automobiles.

▶ **Modern hot-air balloons drift over the Masai Mara game reserve in Tanzania, Africa. They provide a pleasant and silent means of viewing the reserve.**

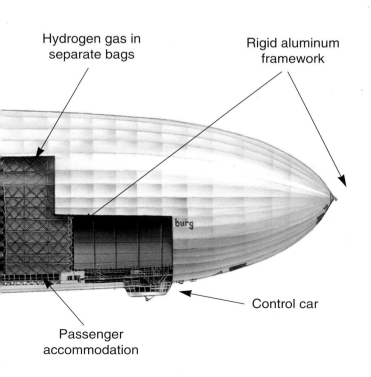

Hydrogen gas in separate bags

Rigid aluminum framework

Control car

Passenger accommodation

**D**uring World War I (1914–18), large German airships, built in a factory started by Count Ferdinand von Zeppelin (1838–1917), dropped bombs on London. By the 1930s passenger airships dwarfing the largest airplanes were cruising across the Atlantic Ocean. However, the airship had a fatal weakness—hydrogen gas catches fire very easily. When the *Hindenburg* burst into flames on landing at Lakehurst, New Jersey, on May 6, 1937, the future for airships as long-distance transportation died with the 36 passengers and crew.

**M**odern airships are used for advertising, pleasure trips, and carrying television cameras. They are filled with helium, a gas that does not burn. Compared to modern airplanes, they are slow and difficult to steer.

# IRON SHIPS

During the 1800s two important changes took place in ship design. First, the large quantities of cheap iron and steel produced by the Industrial Revolution gradually found a use in shipbuilding. Second, steam engines slowly took over from sails as the best way of powering large oceangoing ships.

At first many of the new steamboats had sails as well as engines, in case they ran out of fuel. They had to be big enough to carry enough coal or wood to keep their boilers working between ports, particularly if they were crossing the Atlantic Ocean. They also had paddle wheels, but these large wheels were not very efficient and they sometimes broke in rough seas. In 1843 British engineer Isambard Kingdom Brunel (1806–1859) launched the *Great Britain*, the first large ship to be constructed from iron. She was 320 feet long, weighed 3,300 tons and had a propeller instead of paddle wheels, making her the forerunner of all modern ships.

In 1750 Swiss-born mathematician Daniel Bernoulli (1700–1782) had suggested that steamboats could be driven by the kind of screw used in the ancient world as a water pump. To work well, it had to be turned quickly by a powerful engine. Although it had been tried before, it was not successful until 1836, when English inventor Francis Smith (1808–1874) fitted an Archimedes' screw to a boat. The blades of the screw broke during tests, leaving a stump that was very similar to modern propellers. The stump also made the boat go much faster!

▲ Francis Smith built the propeller steamboat HMS *Rattler* for the British navy in 1843. On April 3, 1845, *Rattler* won a tug-of-war with the paddle-driven sister ship HMS *Alecto*, proving for all time that propellers were much stronger than paddles.

▶ An artist's interpretation of the *Titanic*. When launched, the British passenger ship, *Titanic*, was the longest ship afloat. On its first voyage in April 1912, it struck an iceberg in the North Atlantic and sank. Around 1,500 people died. The funnels on the *Titanic* actually were beige and black.

In 1884 English engineer Charles Parsons (1854–1931) invented a new kind of high-speed steam engine—the steam turbine—and in 1894 he fitted one of these engines to a small boat called *Turbinia*. With a top speed of nearly 40 miles per hour it was faster than any other ship afloat. He demonstrated its speed by making an unofficial visit to a review of the British navy at Spithead in 1897, and he sailed circles around the naval patrol boat sent out to intercept it. Impressed, the navy ordered a turbine-engine ship, the HMS *Viper*, and in 1907 steam turbines were installed in the *Lusitania* and the *Mauretania*. By 1939 there were more than 80 giant turbine-engine passenger liners in service.

 ## BRUNEL: GENIUS ENGINEER

Isambard Kingdom Brunel (1806–59) was born in England, the son of French-born civil engineer Marc Brunel. Isambard designed the Clifton Suspension Bridge near Bristol, England, and in 1833 became chief engineer of England's Great Western Railway.

Isambard Brunel is mostly remembered for his three great steamships, the *Great Western* (1837), which was built to take passengers from the Great Western Railway across the Atlantic Ocean to America, then the *Great Britain* (1843). Finally, in 1858 after many problems, he built the enormous *Great Eastern*. This monster was 19,000 tons, 693 feet long and had a double hull of iron. Built with a propeller, paddle wheels, and sails, the *Great Eastern* was intended to carry four thousand passengers to Australia; but it proved a commercial disaster because the engines burned twice as much coal as Brunel had calculated. The ship made history by laying the first transatlantic telegraph cable and remained the largest ship afloat until it was scrapped in 1889. Worn out by overwork, Brunel died of a stroke on September 15, 1859, shortly before the *Great Eastern*'s maiden voyage.

# THE BICYCLE

Two-wheeled transportation was not taken very seriously before the early 1800s, when the Draisne, upon which a rider sat and pushed with his feet, became popular. It was invented in Germany in 1817 by Baron Drais von Sauerbron.

The first bicycles came to the United States in 1819 and were called velocipedes, or "swift walkers." Three months after they arrived in New York City, they were banned from sidewalks and public places.

▲ The penny farthing was difficult to mount and some cyclists used steps to reach the saddle. In 1878 *Scientific American* stated that the penny farthing was "an ever-saddled horse that eats nothing and requires no care."

In 1839 Kirkpatrick Macmillan, a Scottish blacksmith, made a bicycle driven by foot treadles, but the back-and-forth movement was awkward and tiring. Philip Fischer's crank pedals of the 1850s were much easier on the legs. His design was copied by Ernest Michaux, a French coach builder, who started the first bicycle factory in the 1860s.

Bicycles could be made cheaply in factories. The first bicycles had wooden wheels and were called boneshakers. Women as well as men took to cycling with enthusiasm. In 1870 James Starley (1830–1881), an English inventor, designed the first high-wheeler or penny farthing, and his nephew, John Starley, built the first Rover safety cycle in 1885.

Bicycle riding became much smoother in 1888 when John Boyd Dunlop (1840–1921), a Scottish veterinary surgeon, invented air-filled rubber tires for his son's tricycle wheels. A racing cyclist asked for similar wheels, Dunlop opened a factory, and the "pneumatic tire" took its place in history.

◄ The use of bicycles became the norm in China where, in the 1980s, an estimated 77 million people pedaled to work.

The bicycle is still a cheap ride and healthy exercise, and there are many millions of cyclists worldwide. The latest high-tech racing bikes have streamlined carbon-fiber bodies, disk wheels (fixed to blades instead of forks), and steering columns instead of handlebars. There are miniature bikes, folding bikes, and mountain bikes. The bicycle is a design that works and it will go on working as long as people enjoy pedaling.

▼ This advanced racing bike has revolutionary low steering, a three-spoked front wheel fastened to a single blade, and a rear disk wheel.

# THE AUTOMOBILE

Road vehicles with steam engines were tried out during the 1800s, but they were heavy, needed coal and water, and sometimes blew up. The automobile came about as a result of a series of inventions made between 1860 and 1885. The first was a gas engine, built in 1860 by French inventor Etienne Lenoir (1822–1900). This was a stationary piston engine that burned coal gas, which was used to drive machinery in factories. Nikolaus Otto, a German engineer (1832–1891), developed a more powerful four-stroke gas engine in 1876.

During this time a new fuel became available. Petroleum oil from the United States was refined to make oils suitable for kerosene lamps and to lubricate factory machines. Petroleum spirits, or gasoline, was left over from the refining process. A number of engineers, including Otto, experimented with building engines that used gasoline.

German engineer Gottlieb Daimler had visited Lenoir's factory in 1860 and later worked for Nikolaus Otto developing new engines. In 1882 Daimler left the Otto factory to concentrate on building his own gasoline engine. The first Daimler experimental car was built in 1886, but it was really a horseless carriage fitted with a gasoline engine. It had a top speed of about nine miles per hour. Unknown to Daimler, a neighbor named Karl Benz was about to make history.

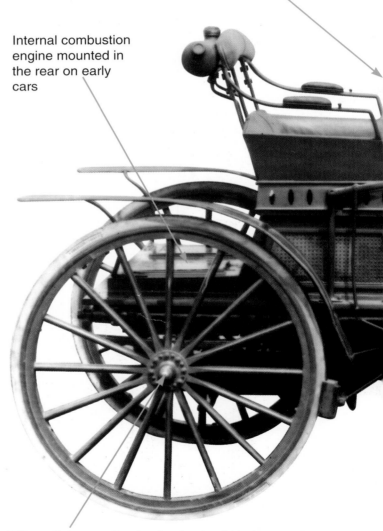

▼ An early Benz four-wheeled car. It has simple lever steering and spoked cart-type wheels. There is no protection for the passengers from bad weather.

Steering tiller

Internal combustion engine mounted in the rear on early cars

Differential gear allowing back wheels to turn at different speeds when turning corners

# BERTA BENZ

Karl Benz had an able partner in his wife Berta. She helped in the design of his car and encouraged him to go on testing it at night, after the commotion its daytime appearances created led to police complaints. Berta pedaled away on her sewing machine to drive a generator that recharged the battery. In August, 1888, she and her sons took the car on its first cross-country trip, from Mannheim to Pforzheim, a distance of some forty miles. She had to buy gasoline from a pharmacy and used one of her garters as insulating tape to repair an electrical fault. The trip was a good test for the car. There were many hurdles still to be overcome—including money, for at first few people were willing to buy a Benz car, or indeed any horseless carriage. But the Benzes persisted, interest slowly grew, and in 1893 they exhibited a Benz car in Chicago, Illinois.

▲ **Karl Benz in 1925, age 81, sitting in the first car he ever built**

Gear shift

Center point steering allowing the front axle to swivel

Solid rubber tires

**K**arl Benz started a business in 1879 making gas engines for factories. Building a car was a hobby that became an obsession. He assembled all the parts— carburetor, electrical ignition, and steering (a lever to the front wheels). A large flywheel was spun to start the engine. The flywheel would keep spinning to store power so that the engine kept running throughout the four-stroke cycle. He borrowed ideas from the bicycle for wheels and gears, and he designed a water cooling system for the engine. On January 29, 1886 Karl Benz was awarded a patent for the Patent Motor Car. By 1900, four thousand three-gear Comfortable models had been sold, and the Benz company was the largest automobile manufacturer in Europe.

# INTO THE AIR

▲ On December 17, 1903, *Flyer* took to the air for the first time.

From earliest times people dreamed of flying like birds. Some would-be fliers leaped from towers wearing wings. Flapping feebly, they crashed to the ground. Yet, while these brave but misguided experiments went on, a practical flying machine was soaring at the end of a line—the kite. The Chinese and Koreans flew kites for fun, probably as early as 1000 B.C. In 1752 American statesman and scientist Benjamin Franklin (1706–1790) flew a kite in a thunderstorm to investigate the nature of lightning.

The kite flies according to the same principles as an airplane. The string tugs it forward (thrust), and the wind pushes it up (lift). Yet no scientist studied kite flying seriously until 1799, when English inventor George Cayley (1773–1857) began designing model gliders—basically winged kites without strings. Cayley figured out a practical theory of flight in a heavier-than-air machine. In 1853 he even sent his reluctant coachman, John Appleby, aloft in a glider. Enthusiasts such as German engineer Otto Lilienthal (1848–1896) soared many times off hillsides showing that a person could fly with fixed wings for a short distance—but Lilienthal died in a gliding accident.

◀ France was the first country to establish an aircraft industry. This poster advertised an air show in Rheims in 1909.

24

Various inventors designed fanciful steam airplanes, but steam engines were far too heavy for flight. The lighter gasoline engine offered a new opportunity. In the United States and Europe, inventors began experimenting with powered gliders. Among them were American brothers Orville (1871–1948) and Wilbur Wright (1867–1912).

On December 17, 1903 the Wrights took their *Flyer* to a lonely stretch of sand hills in North Carolina. Orville lay down at the controls, the propeller whirled, and the flimsy machine lifted into the air. It flew 120 feet. Only five people saw the history-making triumph. The Wrights went on to make much longer flights, but it was some time before the outside world learned of their achievements. In 1905 they offered their invention to the U.S. government, and in 1909 the U.S. Army bought its first airplane.

 ## THE WRIGHT WAY

Orville and Wilbur Wright lived in Dayton, Ohio. Neither went to college or studied engineering. As boys they built a toy helicopter, powered by a rubber band, and made kites. They worked together as adults, first as printers and then running a bicycle shop. In their spare time they built gliders.

The Wright brothers were very methodical. They read reports about the experiences of pioneer glider pilots such as Otto Lilienthal, and they built a wind tunnel to test different wing shapes for their own gliders. Once satisfied, they designed a powered airplane. They built propellers and an engine, and they also designed a system for controlling the plane in the air—by twisting or "warping" the wings. Their successful flight in 1903 did not make newspaper headlines, but by 1912 the Wrights were famous, selling their airplanes in Europe as well as in the United States. Wilbur died of typhoid fever in 1912. Orville sold the business; he died in 1948.

In 1914 airplanes went to war. World War I (1914–18) speeded up air technology dramatically. By 1918 planes could fly at 150 miles per hour, and there were four-engined planes. The British Royal Air Force, which was the first independent air force, had 22,000 aircraft. In 1919 the Atlantic Ocean was crossed by a plane for the first time, and regular passenger services soon followed. In less than 20 years after the Wrights' flight, aviation had made an amazing leap forward.

# SUBMARINES

A number of brave inventors experimented with undersea boats before the submarine became a realistic fighting ship. In 1620 Dutchman Cornelis van Drebbel, working in England for King James I, managed to cross the Thames River in England with a primitive submarine made of greased leather stretched over a wooden frame. Not surprisingly, it leaked. A one-man submarine called *Turtle* was designed in 1776 by American engineer David Bushnell. It was used in an unsuccessful attack on the British warship *Eagle* in New York Harbor during the American Revolution (1775–1783).

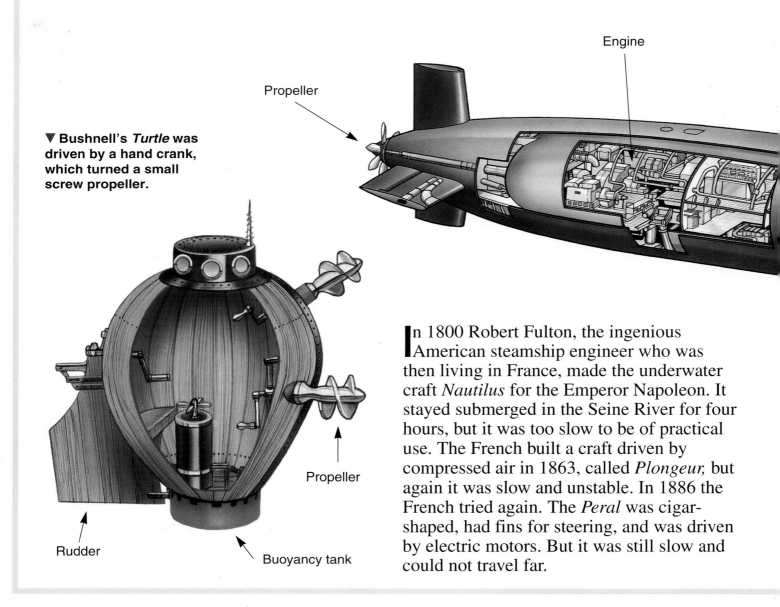

▼ Bushnell's *Turtle* was driven by a hand crank, which turned a small screw propeller.

Engine

Propeller

Propeller

Rudder

Buoyancy tank

In 1800 Robert Fulton, the ingenious American steamship engineer who was then living in France, made the underwater craft *Nautilus* for the Emperor Napoleon. It stayed submerged in the Seine River for four hours, but it was too slow to be of practical use. The French built a craft driven by compressed air in 1863, called *Plongeur,* but again it was slow and unstable. In 1886 the French tried again. The *Peral* was cigar-shaped, had fins for steering, and was driven by electric motors. But it was still slow and could not travel far.

Finally in 1900 Irish-born American John P. Holland (1840–1914) successfully showed *Holland VI* to the U.S. Navy on and under the Potomac River. It had a range of 500 miles on the surface and 24 miles underwater. It could fire torpedoes large enough to sink a battleship and had a periscope that could be raised to view the scene above the water. Here was a fighting machine to interest the navies of the world.

During World War I submarines sank many cargo ships as well as warships. During World War II (1939-1945) the balance in the deadly undersea war first favored the German submarines, or U-boats, but the development of sonar and radar tilted the advantage toward the hunters on the surface—ships and aircraft.

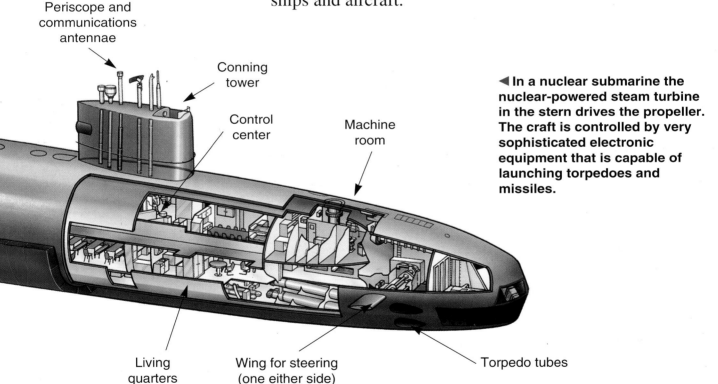

Periscope and communications antennae

Conning tower

Control center

Machine room

◄ In a nuclear submarine the nuclear-powered steam turbine in the stern drives the propeller. The craft is controlled by very sophisticated electronic equipment that is capable of launching torpedoes and missiles.

Living quarters

Wing for steering (one either side)

Torpedo tubes

In 1954 the U.S. Navy launched *Nautilus,* the world's first nuclear submarine. Today, nuclear submarines are the most powerful naval warships. They can be very big (weighing up to 20,000 tons) and are whale-shaped to reduce water resistance. The nuclear reactor heats steam to drive turbine engines. Underwater, a nuclear submarine can travel as fast as most surface ships. Sucking in air through snorkel tubes, it can circle the world without surfacing.

# THE ROAD REVOLUTION

Many people were suspicious of automobiles when they were first invented. In Great Britain the "red flag" law of 1865 forced all self-propelled vehicles to crawl behind a walker with a red flag—this was the first speed limit. In France people were more sympathetic and racing on public highways became accepted. This gave French manufacturers a great advantage because they could test cars at high speed. French inventors such as Emile Levassor made cars more comfortable, with covered roofs and, after 1895, air-filled tires. Levassor moved the engine to the front of the car and made other mechanical improvements. By 1900 all the main features of the automobile had been developed.

▼ The Model T was produced in black because one of Henry Ford's engineers discovered that black paint dried faster than any other color. Today the Model T is highly prized by people who collect vintage cars.

In both Europe and the United States cars were built by hand, and so were very expensive. Only rich people could afford them. In the United States, however, the numbers of cars began to increase despite the high price. In 1902 there was one car for every one and a half million U.S. citizens. By 1907 there was one for every eight hundred. Henry Ford (1863–1947) had been making cars in Detroit since 1903. He was convinced cars could be made more cheaply and in October 1908 he launched his Model T—the immortal "Tin Lizzie." The Model T was very basic, strong, and light. It was built for inexperienced drivers and rough roads and cost less than half the price of other cars. It was made from standard parts, and by the summer of 1913 Ford had devised a production line that rolled off two thousand cars a month.

 # HENRY FORD

Henry Ford was born on a farm in Michigan. He left school when he was 15 to work as an apprentice in a machine shop. He built his first car in 1893 when he was 30 years old. It was the only car in Detroit, and Ford drove it one thousand miles before selling it.

He was employed by the local electric company, who offered him a promotion if he would stop tinkering with his "gas buggies." Instead he left his job in 1899 to form his own company in Detroit, and later the Ford Motor Company in 1903. After a number of years of experiment and struggle, he finally built the Model T in 1908. In the first year, with $100,000 of capital, 10,607 cars were built. By 1927 there were more than 15 million Model Ts on the road, and the company had $700 million in the bank.

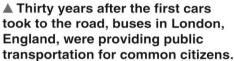

▲ Thirty years after the first cars took to the road, buses in London, England, were providing public transportation for common citizens.

▶ Modern highways, like this one in Spessart, Germany, allow people to reach places that were not easily accessible 50 years ago.

Gradually roads improved to keep pace with the increasing numbers of vehicles. Buses, electric streetcars, and trolleycars provided public transportation for people without cars, which was still the majority in industrialized countries before World War II. In the 1920s and 1930s the first superhighways for fast cars and trucks were built in Germany and Italy. During the 1950s car ownership increased rapidly, particularly in Europe and North America. Highways now crisscross most countries of the world. The car has changed old cities, created new suburbs, and altered the way people live.

Today the emphasis in new car design is on safety, and the production line is operated by robots. In 1909 French chemist Edouard Benedictus sandwiched celluloid between two sheets of glass to make safety glass. Today many windshields are made of glass laminated with plastic, seat belts are mandatory, steering wheels collapse on impact, and airbags inflate to protect drivers. Car bodies are designed with crumple zones which absorb the energy of impact.

# ELECTRIC AND DIESEL TRAINS

In 1879 German inventor Werner von Siemens (1816–1892) showed a small electric locomotive at the Berlin Trades Exhibition, and in 1881 a Berlin tramway was run on electricity. The Volks Electric Railway opened along Brighton Beach, southern England, in 1883, and in the same year the Giant's Causeway and Portrush Railway opened in Northern Ireland. Other small electric railroads swiftly started up across Europe and the United States. The Baltimore and Ohio Railroad opened the world's first main line electric railroad through a tunnel under the city of Baltimore in 1895.

Electric locomotives were lighter, cleaner, and more efficient than steam engines, but the method of supplying the electricity to the trains and the high voltages involved in transmitting the current efficiently along the railroad lines were problems. Most European railroads were quick to develop electrification for long distance travel, but the United States and Great Britain tended to keep to steam.

◄ A train heads out of Paris, France, on its way to the Channel Tunnel. Specially built for the Paris–London run, Channel Tunnel trains can run on both British and French tracks.

The diesel engine was invented in 1897 by Rudolf Diesel, a German mechanical engineer (1858–1913). He designed an engine that didn't need spark plugs and that burned cheap oil instead of the more expensive gasoline. It was shown at an exhibition in Munich in 1898, and its inventor soon became a millionaire. The first diesel locomotive ran in 1912 on the Prussian–Hessian State Railway in Germany, and by 1934 massive diesel locomotives were hauling freight and passenger trains across the United States.

By the 1950s diesel and electric trains were shunting steam off the main lines and into history. No steam train ever ran faster than 125 miles per hour—a record set by the *Mallard* in Great Britain in 1938. The French *Trés Grande Vitesse* electric express daily produce an average speed of just over 131 miles per hour on the Paris–Lyon run, and these superfast expresses now compete with airlines on the main intercity routes in Europe.

Today, railroads run diesel or electric trains, though in some parts of the world steam still survives. The decision as to which type of power to use is based on the cost of installation, the distance to be covered, the number of passengers traveling, and the competition provided by other means of transportation.

▲ A powerful diesel locomotive moves freight through a train yard in Oregon.

 # SUBWAYS

To solve the problem of building railroads in crowded cities, nineteenth-century engineers went underground. The first underground railroad was London's Metropolitan Railway, completed in 1863. Its tunnels were covered trenches, rather than deep tunnels. Steam and smoke from the steam locomotives filled the tunnels and enveloped passengers waiting in stations. The locomotives were fitted with "smoke-eating" devices, that did not really work. In 1890 the City and South London Railway was the first real subway. It used electric trains, putting an end to the smoky tunnels. The first subway in America was built in New York City in 1904.

The track circuit system, automatically controlling signals on sections of track, was invented in the United States in 1872, and ensured that trains on the same line but only a minute or so apart did not collide. Modern subways are almost completely automated. Passengers can buy tickets from a machine; electronic gates read the ticket; trains are run by remote-control along computer-monitored tracks. But passengers still like to see an engineer in charge of the train.

# CIVIL AIRCRAFT

In the 1920s aircraft engineers realized that if an aircraft had a streamlined shape, it would have a greater speed because there would be less drag from the air. By 1935 aircraft had become all-metal monoplanes with several propellers and landing gear that tucked inside the plane during flight. They were fast and comfortable and delivered passengers, mail, and other cargo around the world.

The jet engine was a development of the gas turbine engine, and it made planes go even faster. In the 1930s two young engineers, Frank Whittle (1907– ) in Great Britain and Pabst von Ohain (1911– ) in Germany, working separately, produced jet engines that did not need propellers. Ohain fitted his new engine into a Heinkel HE 178 and the first jet plane took to the air on August 27, 1939—though it was not a particularly inspiring aircraft. Whittle's turbojet engine was far more impressive. On May 15, 1941 a Gloster E28/39 took off and achieved a top speed of 337 miles per hour. When fitted with a more powerful turbojet the Gloster managed 437 miles per hour. As tests continued they proved that jet engines worked even better at higher speeds and greater altitudes.

▲ A Gloster E28/39 fitted with an early version of the jet engine

After World War II, the United States, the Soviet Union, Great Britain, and France competed to build faster and bigger jet planes. In 1957 about 90 million people traveled on the world's airlines. When the American Boeing company launched the Boeing 707 in 1958, it was quickly followed by a whole family of Boeing planes. During the 1960s the air travel industry developed rapidly worldwide, and by 1971 Boeing designs accounted for 2,200 of the 3,600 jet airliners then in service. The massive Boeing 747 entered service in January 1970. With its turbofan engines it was quieter than previous jets and its huge capacity—up to 490 passengers—made it cost effective at the time.

The supersonic Anglo–French Concorde went into service in 1976, transporting up to one hundred passengers across the Atlantic Ocean in about three hours—most of the time at twice the speed of sound. Advanced in its day, but very expensive, Concorde has not been a commercial success. Airlines prefer bigger if slower passenger carriers, like the Boeing 757 and European Airbus.

◀ Concorde on the runway at London's Heathrow Airport, with a Boeing 747 jumbo jet behind

Air travel is now extremely popular. In 1993, at Chicago's O'Hare Airport, there were over 65 million passenger arrivals and departures.

 ## GLAMOROUS GLENNIS

On October 14, 1947 at Muroc Air Force Base, California, the rocket-powered Bell X-1 flew faster than the speed of sound. The plane was flown by Air Force Captain Charles E. Yeager and named *Glamorous Glennis* after Yeager's wife. As a plane approaches the speed of sound (about 740 miles an hour) it passes through a shock wave, and there is a loud bang called a sonic boom. Some experts believed the aircraft would be destroyed by the shock, but the fear proved to be without foundation. It was then only a matter of time before aircraft were designed to carry passengers at supersonic speed.

# HELICOPTERS

Italian artistic genius Leonardo da Vinci (1452–1519) sketched designs in his notebook for a machine similar to a helicopter. It had a propellerlike spinning rotor made from iron wire and cloth. As a child he may have played with a Chinese top, a flying toy with feather rotors that had been known for at least two thousand years before it reached Europe in the Middle Ages. Leonardo's machine would probably have flown had there been an engine to supply the power needed to turn the propeller, but a suitable engine was about 350 years in the future.

▲ The helicopter is ideal for air-sea rescue because of its ability to hover over a ship, lower rescuers, and lift off people in danger.

▲ Igor Sikorsky at the controls of his VS-300 helicopter on September 14, 1939.

The first helicopter to fly steadily and well was built in 1936 by Heinrich Focke of Germany. It had twin rotor blades set on outriggers. In 1939 Igor Sikorsky (1889–1972), a Russian engineer working in the United States, designed a helicopter with just one rotor blade. He suggested that if the rotor blades could be tilted to "bite" into the air, a pilot could make the helicopter fly forward, backward, or sideways. To keep the aircraft from spinning around as the rotor turned (this twisting force is called torque), a second smaller rotor on the tail spun vertically. This countered the torque and also helped steer the helicopter. In 1942 an improved version of the VS-300 helicopter, the R-4, went into production. All modern single-rotor helicopters are based on the R-4 design.

▲ A Bell-Boeing V22 Osprey photographed in June 1993. The Osprey has a tilt-rotor design. It flies more like a fixed-wing airplane, but it does not need a long runway.

Since those early days, helicopters have become bigger, faster, and indispensable. The first air-sea rescue by helicopter was in 1945 off Long Island, New York when two men stranded for 16 hours on a wrecked tanker in a gale were winched off. Adopted by armies and navies around the world to support troops and hunt for submarines, helicopters also have a multitude of commercial uses, from supplying oil rigs to finding shipping lanes through ice fields. They are also used to monitor traffic in cities. As flying cranes they perform jobs that would otherwise be extremely difficult: in 1962 a Royal Air Force helicopter placed the cross on top of the new Coventry Cathedral in England.

For passenger transportation, helicopters are noisy and use too much fuel, but there is no doubt about their advantage over fixed-wing aircraft. Only the Harrier jump jet, using swiveling nozzles to direct the jet thrust from its engines, can match the helicopter for maneuverability. Tilt-wing aircraft, which take off like a helicopter and then tilt their wings (and engines) to fly forward, are assured of a future—if they can be made to fly quietly.

# BIG CARRIERS

The more goods that can be moved on one vehicle, the cheaper the transportation per item. This simple piece of economics has caused engineers to build bigger—bigger trucks, bigger planes, bigger ships. Brunel's *Great Eastern* at 19,000 tons was too big for 1858—it was out of step with the technology of its time. By the 1900s, the world was ready for mass transport, and in the 1930s shipyards were launching passenger liners of 40,000 tons and up which remained economical until passenger jet aircraft swept them aside in the 1960s. The *Queen Mary,* at 81,237 tons, was launched in 1934 and taken out of service 33 years later. The ship could carry 2,000 passengers.

► Natural gas is carried in huge refrigerated tankers. At −260°F the gas is liquid but some does evaporate into the air space inside the tanks. This evaporated gas can be siphoned off and used as a boiler fuel for the ship.

The first modern-style oil tanker was the *Gluckauf,* built in 1886 at 3,000 tons. It was a dwarf compared to the *Hellas Fos,* the largest tanker and ship of any kind in service one hundred years later. The *Hellas Fos,* weighing 555,051 tons, is a steam turbine tanker built in 1979. Since the 1950s oil fuel has been in huge demand for cars and power plants. This has encouraged shippers to build giant tankers. Before the 1950s cargo ships were smaller than passenger ships. Few were more than 40,000 tons. Huge tankers are too large to pass through the Suez or Panama canals, but they carry enormous cargoes, and the cost savings compensate for longer travel times. Ships carrying bulk cargoes such as natural gas and metal ores can be as large as 350,000 tons, like the *Berge Stahl,* which was first launched at Ulsan, South Korea, in 1986.

Costs are also reduced if less time is spent loading and unloading the cargo. In 1955 the tanker *Ideal X* was converted to carry containers on her decks. Today custom-built container ships transport manufactured goods around the world, spending a minimum amount of time in port. At a container port, such as the Rotterdam-Europoort in the Netherlands, the containers arrive on trucks. They are lifted off by cranes and piled up in computer-controlled waiting areas along the docks. When a container ship comes into port, one load of containers can be quickly replaced by another.

◀ **A container arrives by truck at the modern docks in Baltimore, Maryland. In the background a container ship is being loaded.**

In 1900 most overland freight was carried by train. Freight began to transfer from trains to trucks in the 1920s, after World War I had boosted truck production and brought improvements in truck size and reliability. After the 1950s the new, faster highways were soon filled by new and bigger trucks, some weighing 50 tons when fully loaded. Specialized trucks can be gigantic: the world's biggest dump truck has a loaded weight of 549 tons. Many trucks are built to carry containers to and from ports. The engine and driver's cab form a detachable tractor unit, hitched to a trailer on which containers are carried. Most big trucks have diesel engines and are fitted with streamlined wind deflectors to cut air resistance and thus save fuel and money.

# ROCKETS AND SPACECRAFT

▲ On April 12, 1961, Russian astronaut Yuri Gagarin became the first person to travel in space. A giant rocket put his spacecraft, *Vostok 1*, into orbit around the Earth. The flight lasted 118 minutes. He made one complete circuit of the Earth and landed safely less than six miles from the calculated point.

Rockets were used by the Chinese about 2,000 years ago as fireworks or weapons, and rockets were in use in Europe by the 1300s. A rocket is a cylinder packed with fuel. When the fuel burns, gases rush out of the bottom, propelling the cylinder high into the air. During the 1800s science-fiction writers imagined people flying into space, either fired from cannon as in Jules Verne's book *From the Earth to the Moon* (1865) or inside rockets. Scientists were much more skeptical. Many dismissed spaceflight as impossible. A Russian teacher, Konstantin Tsiolkovsky (1857–1935), wrote out the theory of space-rocket flight in 1903. His work inspired physicists such as American Robert Hutchings Goddard (1882–1945), and by 1926 Goddard successfully launched his first rocket from a desert in New Mexico.

The first long-range rocket, the V2, was built as a bomb-carrying weapon during World War II by German engineer Wernher von Braun (1912–1977). It had a range of about 200 miles, rose 60 miles in the air, and descended at several times the speed of sound. After the war, captured V2s and German scientists were taken to the United States and the Soviet Union. In 1957 a powerful Russian rocket put the first artificial satellite, *Sputnik 1*, into orbit around Earth; and on April 12, 1961 a rocket carried Yuri Gagarin, the first person to fly into space, into orbit.

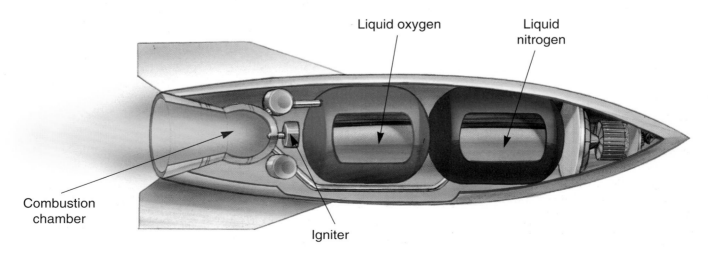

Liquid oxygen

Liquid nitrogen

Combustion chamber

Igniter

International prestige then fueled the space race. President John F. Kennedy (1917–1963) announced the Apollo space program, which aimed to put an American on the moon by the end of the 1960s. Huge sums of money were spent. In July 1969 a Saturn V rocket, designed by von Braun's team, launched *Apollo 11*, and American astronauts Neil Armstrong and Edwin Aldrin became the first human beings to set foot on the moon. Since then ten other astronauts have visited the moon—all of them Americans.

Multistage rockets like Saturn V can be used only once because most of the rocket is destroyed during the escape from the Earth's gravity. The first of the space shuttle fleet, *Columbia*, was launched from Cape Canaveral, Florida, in 1981. Space shuttles are a combination of rocket, space station, and glider and are still the world's only reusable spacecraft. In 1986 the Soviet Union launched the Mir space station. It is an orbiting laboratory visited regularly by teams of astronauts, some of whom have spent more than a year in orbit. In June 1995 space shuttle *Atlantis* made a significant advance by successfully docking with the Mir space station. A new international space station is planned, to continue research into human flight.

▲ Space shuttle *Columbia* climbs away from the launchpad on June 5, 1991. A shuttle travels into space strapped to a huge fuel tank and driven by two powerful boosters. First the boosters and then the fuel tank fall away before the shuttle reaches orbit. When returning to Earth, the shuttle makes a controlled landing on a runway, like a glider.

◀ Many rockets use liquid nitrogen as a fuel. This is mixed with liquid oxygen in the combustion chamber, where the nitrogen ignites explosively. As gases rush out the exhaust, the rocket is propelled forward with an equal and opposite force.

The space programs have spawned a vast space industry. Factories build communications, weather, spy, and navigation satellites. They also provide spacecraft, rocket engines, computers, space suits, special space foods, and life support systems for astronauts working in space. However, although robotic space probes have been sent to all of the planets in the solar system (with the exception of Pluto), extensive space travel by human beings still remains highly unlikely at the present time.

# FUTURE TRANSPORTATION

Kreislauf der Nat

Inventions made in the last two hundred years—railroads, cars, airplanes—have enabled people to move farther and faster than ever before. Yet the telecommunications revolution of the last ten years may, in future, make many journeys unnecessary. More people may work from home, shop by telephone, communicate globally via Internet and video telephone. But goods will still have to be manufactured and raw materials, goods, and people will still have to be moved around the world.

▲ One of the six natural-gas-powered buses, which in 1995 were undergoing trials in Trondheim, Norway

Science, technology, need, economics, and governments will shape the transportation systems of the next century. We need cleaner, more efficient vehicles to reduce pollution and environmental damage. We need to conserve Earth's resources and develop new alternative sources of energy to preserve Earth's precious stocks of oil, gas, and coal. We once hoped that nuclear power would provide limitless energy, but it is not limitless, cheap, or risk-free. We are beginning to make better use of wind power, ocean tides, and the heat of the sun. We still need to waste less and preserve more.

▼ The hydrofoil is not a new invention. The first commercial hydrofoil went into service in 1956, between Sicily and the Italian mainland. Because the craft rides mostly above the water, friction is reduced, allowing it to move faster. However, the foils damage easily and as the weight of the craft increases, the power required to drive it at high speed increases dramatically.

▲ At the Frankfurt Motor Show in 1991, BMW exhibited its electric car, the BMW E1. Electric cars have limited range and power because they are battery-driven. Electric cars are not new. Manufacturers have been experimenting with them for 30 years. The problem is the batteries: they need to be light, long-lasting, and easily rechargeable.

The car is a worldwide symbol of status and personal mobility. Car manufacture is a huge industry that provides many people with a living. Yet motor vehicles cause much of the congestion and pollution that invade our large cities and highways. Electric cars are much quieter and cleaner, but they cannot travel far or fast or move heavy loads. To protect our well-being, we need to both change the way we live and clean up the exhaust gases produced by our transportation. We need to provide as much personal mobility and freedom as possible. We also need to provide effective ways of moving goods and people around the world.

# CHRONOLOGY OF ADVANCE

Here are some of the people, discoveries, inventions, and improvements that have helped shape the transportation we use today.

**Middle East, Egypt, China** The wheel (inventor unknown) came into being in about 3500 B.C., before the cart or the tame horse. Domestic animals such as donkeys, oxen, camels, and dogs were used to carry and drag loads long before then.

**Mediterranean** About 3000 B.C. Egyptian, and later Phoenician and Greek, sailors ventured to sea in sailing ships to explore and trade.

**Ancient Romans** From the first century A.D. the Romans built stone-topped roads across their empire, mainly for the army but also for trade.

**Ancient Chinese** By about A.D. 1100 the Chinese had built canals and invented the kite, the gunpowder rocket, and the magnetic compass. Chinese junks were the largest cargo ships of their time.

**Leonardo da Vinci** An Italian artist and inventor (1452–1519) who sketched various machines including a helicopter and an armored fighting vehicle—none of which was ever built.

▲ Robert Fulton

**Isaac Newton** A British scientist (1642–1727) who worked out a theory of gravitation and described the three laws of force and motion, published in his book, *Philosophiae Naturalis Principia Mathematica,* in 1687.

**James Watt** A Scottish engineer (1736–1819) who improved the steam engine, making it more powerful, and converted its motion from vertical to rotary.

**Joseph Montgolfier** A French papemaker (1740–1810) who, with his brother **Etienne** (1745–1799), in 1783 built the first hot-air balloon to fly with human passengers.

**Richard Trevithick** An English engineer (1771–1833) who built steam-engined vehicles for road and rail, proving that steam was a new power source for transportation.

**George Stephenson** A British engineer (1781–1848), who designed the locomotive for the world's first passenger steam train. His son **Robert** (1803–1859) was also a civil engineer.

**Robert Fulton** An American inventor (1765–1815) who built a submarine in 1800, and also the steamboat *Clermont,* which ran the first public steamboat service in 1807.

**George Cayley** A British scientist (1771–1857) who worked on the theory of glider flight, built a model glider, and produced a larger machine that could carry a human being. His studies inspired later pioneers such as Otto Lilienthal of Germany.

**Isambard Kingdom Brunel** A British engineer (1806–1859) who built tunnels and bridges and the Great Western Railway. He is best known for his three remarkable steamships: the *Great Western* (1837), the *Great Britain* (1843), and the *Great Eastern* (1858).

**Etienne Lenoir** A French engineer (1822–1900) who invented a stationary engine that burned coal gas—the first internal combustion engine.

**Werner von Siemens** A German industrialist and inventor (1816–1892) who developed electric railroads, lighting, and telegraphs. His brother **William** (1823–1883) invented a new steelmaking process.

**James Starley** A British engineer (1830–1881) who built sewing machines and improved bicycles with gears. He began building Ariel bicycles in 1871.

**John Boyd Dunlop** A Scottish inventor (1840–1921) who was the first manufacturer of inflated rubber tires.

**Charles Parsons** A British engineer (1854–1931) who built the first steam turbine engine for ships. Steam turbines were later used in power plants to generate electricity.

**Gottlieb Daimler** A German engineer (1834–1900) who built a motorcycle and a car in 1886 and was one of the pioneers of automobile development.

**Karl Benz** A German engineer (1844–1929) who built the world's first automobile driven by a gasoline engine. He and Gottlieb Daimler were the fathers of the automobile.

**Ferdinand von Zeppelin** A German engineer (1838–1917) who built airships, which from 1900 to the 1930s bore his name and were the largest ever made.

**John P. Holland** An American engineer (1840–1914) who built the first reliable submarine in 1897. It had gasoline and electric engines and was bought by both the British and the U.S. navies.

**Rudolf Diesel** A German engineer (1858–1913) who turned from refrigerators to engines, developing the oil-fueled engine that bears his name.

**Wilbur Wright** An American inventor (1867–1912) who with his brother **Orville** (1871–1948) ran a bicycle shop in Dayton, Ohio. Self-taught, they built the *Flyer,* which in 1903 made the first flight by a winged, heavier-than-air machine under its own power.

▲ **Henry Ford with his first car**

**Henry Ford** An American industrialist (1863–1947) who built the first mass-produced car, the Model T, on an assembly line. The car was produced at a price common citizens could afford, was robust, and was easy to drive. He later built aircraft and tractors.

**Frank Whittle** A British engineer (1907– ) who developed the theory of the jet engine and patented a gas-turbine jet in 1930. His engine was ground-tested in 1937 but was not put in a plane until 1941.

**Igor Sikorsky** A Russian inventor (1889–1972) who emigrated to the United States in 1919. He founded the Sikorsky Aero Engineering Corporation in 1923 and designed the first single-rotor helicopter in 1939.

**Robert Watson-Watt** A British scientist (1892–1973) who developed radar (RAdio Detection And Ranging) in the 1930s. It was first used to detect enemy bombers during World War II, but has since become an essential navigation aid for ships and aircraft.

**Sergei Korolyov** A Ukrainian-born engineer (1906–1966) who developed the Soviet Union's rocket program. Working on captured German V2 rockets in the late 1940s, he built the huge rockets that gave the Soviet Union an early lead in the space race. His Vostok rockets launched the first space satellites and the world's first astronaut, Yuri Gagarin.

# GLOSSARY

**Airship**  An aircraft filled with a lighter-than-air gas, such as helium or hydrogen. Unlike balloons, they have engines that drive propellers and are usually cigar-shaped rather than spherical.

**Apollo**  The name given to the American moon-flight program. Seven Apollo moon landings were made from 1969 to 1972.

**Archimedes' screw**  A spiral screw turned by a crank inside a casing, originally used to lift water for irrigation. It is thought to have been invented by Greek mathematician Archimedes (c. 287–212 B.C.).

**Battery**  An electrical cell that uses chemical reactions to make electricity.

**Carburetor**  The part of a gasoline engine that mixes air with gas to form an explosive vapor. The vapor is let into the cylinder, where it is ignited by a spark from a spark plug.

**Carrack**  Sailing ship of the 1400s, with three masts carrying square and lateen sails.

**Coal gas**  Gas made by distilling or heating coal. It is mainly methane, hydrogen, and carbon monoxide. Used for heating and lighting from the 1800s, it has now been largely replaced by natural gas.

**Container**  A large metal box in which factory goods are packed before shipment. The container can be carried by road or rail, in large aircraft, or on the decks of special ships. The cargo remains inside until the container reaches its destination.

**Crankshaft**  In a steam or gasoline engine, this is linked by connecting rods to the pistons. The sliding rods convert one kind of motion to another. As the pistons go up and down, the crankshaft is turned around and around.

**Cylinder**  A hollow tube in an engine, inside which a piston moves up and down with a pumping action.

**Diesel engine**  An internal combustion engine in which fuel is ignited by hot compressed air, not by spark plugs. It is named after its inventor, Rudolf Diesel.

**Distributor**  The part of a gasoline engine that sends high-voltage electrical current from the coil to each spark plug.

**Economics**  The science that studies the production, distribution, and consumption of wealth.

**Expansion**  Spreading out or taking up more space. Gases and many other substances expand when heated.

**Flywheel**  A spinning wheel fixed to the crankshaft of a gasoline engine. It stores enough energy during the power stroke to carry the crankshaft through the other strokes (*see* **Stroke**). Flywheels were also used in steam engines to do the same job.

**Friction**  A force created when two objects or substances rub together. Lubrication (oiling or greasing moving parts) and bearings (metal balls rolling between the parts) help to reduce friction.

**Galleon**  A type of sailing ship developed in the 1500s, which was larger and faster than the earlier carrack. Galleons had three or four masts. Their design changed little from 1600 to 1800.

**Gas**  One of the three forms of matter (the others are solid and liquid). A gas has no fixed shape or volume and expands to fill any container.

**Gasoline**  A fuel burned in car engines that is a mixture of chemicals called hydrocarbons, made from refined petroleum oil.

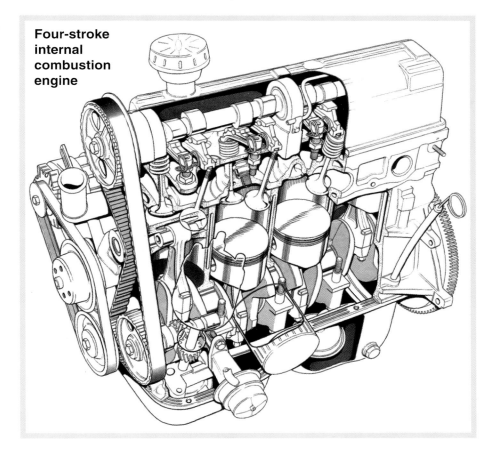

**Four-stroke internal combustion engine**

**Gauge** The distance between inside edges of train track. Standard rail gauge in the United States, Great Britain, and most of Europe is 4 feet 8½ inches.

**Gears** Wheels with cogs or teeth that mesh with one another.

**Glider** An aircraft with wings but no engine. The glider is heavier than air and cannot take off on its own. It has to be launched by being towed or catapulted, but can then gain height by soaring on rising currents of warm air. Model gliders and gliders from which a person dangled (like the modern hang glider) were used in early aviation experiments in the 1800s.

**Gravity** Force of attraction between objects. The planets and the stars pull nearby objects to them, toward their centers.

**Hull** The main body of a ship. Modern hulls are made from welded steel sections.

**Ignition system** An electrical circuit that uses power from a battery to make a spark. This explodes the fuel mixture inside a gasoline engine.

**Industrial Revolution** A change in society by which many people move from agriculture to factory work. It began in England in the second half of the eighteenth century and spread to the rest of Europe and the United States in the nineteenth century.

**Internal combustion engine** An engine that burns gasoline or fuel oil inside a cylinder to produce motion that is transmitted by a shaft to drive wheels or propellers.

**Internet** A worldwide computer web through which users can send and receive information by way of telephone lines and satellites.

**Jet** A fast-moving stream of air, gas, or water. A jet engine burns fuel and shoots out hot exhaust gases; this force pushes the engine in the opposite direction.

**Kayak** A type of canoe used by Arctic Inuit people. It is made from sealskin stretched over a frame and is propelled by a double paddle.

**Lateen sail** A triangular sail first used by Arab and Asian sailors. In the 1400s it was copied by European shipbuilders.

**Liquid fuels** The preferred fuels for space rockets, although solid-fuel boosters are used during launching of some rockets. The liquid is a chemical mixture. The Saturn V moon rocket burned a mixture of liquid oxygen and liquid hydrogen.

**Nuclear power** The harnessing of the energy of nuclear fission (atom splitting) in a reactor so that it can be used to do work. The energy can be used to heat water to make steam to drive turbine engines, as in a nuclear power station or nuclear submarine.

**Patent** A document in which an inventor describes a new invention, and claims sole rights to make, use, and sell it.

**Periscope** An optical instrument that has a tube with reflecting mirrors on either end. It can be raised from a submarine underwater to give a view above the surface.

**Pneumatic tire** Air-filled tires, available from the 1880s. The first bicycles and cars had wooden or metal wheels with hard rims and later solid rubber tires.

**Propeller** Device with blades set at angles around a shaft. All airplanes had spinning propellers before 1939. Ships are driven by large propellers, which turn more slowly in the water. Some hovercraft also have propellers.

**Radar** This stands for RAdio Detection And Ranging. It is a device that sends out radio waves and picks up reflected echoes from objects. It is used for air and sea navigation, military target detection, and air-traffic control.

**Rudder** A vertical blade fastened to the stern of a ship. When the rudder is turned, the ship turns left or right.

**Snorkel** A breathing tube in a submarine that sticks up above the water while the rest of the submarine is submerged. It takes in fresh air and gets rid of stale air and fumes.

**Sonar** SOund Navigation And Ranging. It is a device for detecting underwater objects through reflected sound waves.

**Space station** A permanent base in orbit around Earth that is assembled from sections brought up by rocket. It is used by visiting astronauts for scientific and engineering research in space.

**Spark plug** A device used in gasoline engines to make a spark jump across a gap when a strong electric current passes through it. The spark ignites a fuel and air mixture.

**Steam engine** An engine in which water is heated in a boiler to make steam. The steam is then used at high pressure to drive pistons linked by rods to the drive wheels of factory machines or vehicles.

**Stroke** The movement of a piston inside the cylinder of an engine. A four-stroke engine has four sequences: suction when fuel enters the cylinder; compression when it is squeezed; ignition when it is ignited;

▲ The Mir space station has been in orbit around the Earth since 1986. It is visited by teams of astronauts who carry out experiments in space.

and exhaust that removes the waste gases.

**Transmission system** A series of simple machines that transmits or links the motion of the engine to the drive wheels. The up-and-down action of the pistons is converted into the rotary motion of the wheels.

**Turbine** An engine in which a flow of steam, water, or gas spins blades fixed to a shaft. Gas turbines are used in ships and jet planes. Steam turbines are used in ships.

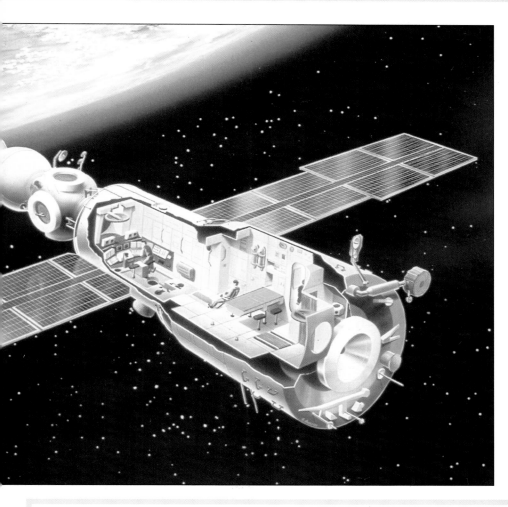

**Vacuum** A space from which air and other substances are removed. A train's vacuum brake is held poised by very low air pressure (a near vacuum) and is engaged when air is allowed in.

**Valve** A device that lets a substance flow one way only; for example, an inlet valve lets the air-fuel mixture into the cylinder of a gasoline engine.

**Wind tunnel** A device in which cars, aircraft, or rocket designs in model form are tested. A fan blows air around the model, so that the model's behavior at different speeds can be studied.

# FURTHER READING

**Books**

Cooper, Alan. *Rail Travel*. World on the Move. New York: Thomson Learning, 1993.

Davies, Eryl. *Transport: On Land, Road and Rail*. Timelines. New York: Franklin Watts, 1992.

Gardner, Robert. *Transportation*. Yesterday's Science, Today's Technology. New York: Twenty-First Century Books, 1994.

Grady, Sean M. *Ships: Crossing the World's Oceans*. The Encyclopedia of Discovery and Invention. San Diego: Lucent Books, 1992.

Graham, Ian. *Transportation*. Facing the Future. Milwaukee: Raintree Steck-Vaughn, 1992.

Immell, Myra H. *Automobiles: Connecting People and Places*. The Encyclopedia of Discovery and Invention. San Diego: Lucent Books, 1994.

Italia, Robert. *Great Auto Makers and Their Cars*. Profiles. Oliver Press, MN 1993.

Lambert, Mark. *Transportation*. Young Geographer. New York: Thomson Learning, 1993.

Macaulay, David. *The Way Things Work*. Boston: Houghton Mifflin, 1988.

Perry, Philippa. *Mega Machines*. Info Adventure. New York: Thomson Learning, 1995.

*The Visual Dictionary of Flight*. Eyewitness Visual Dictionaries. New York: Dorling Kindersley, 1992.

Wilson, Anthony. *The Dorling Kindersley Visual Timeline of Transportation*. New York: Dorling Kindersley, 1995.

**Magazines**

*Car and Driver*, 1633 Broadway, New York, NY 10019

*Discover*, 114 Fifth Avenue, New York, NY 10011

*Popular Mechanics*, Box 7170, Red Oak, IA 51591

*Popular Science*, Box 5100, Harlan, IA 51563

*Scientific American*, 415 Madison Avenue, New York, NY 10017

# INDEX